King vulture

Those Voracious Vultures

Marta Magellan

Illustrations by Steve Weaver

Photographs by

James Gersing and Ron Magill

Pineapple Press, Inc.
Sarasota, Florida

Photo Credits

Andean condor, turkey, and juvenile king vulture photos by James Gersing (questions 4, 5, 8, 10, 11, 12, 17, 18, 20, and author photo); African vultures and adult king vulture photos by Ron Magill (cover, frontispiece, questions 1, 2, 3, 6, 14, and 16; yellow-headed and black vulture photos by Marta Magellan (questions 13, 15, 19); Eurasian and Lappet-headed vultures (question 7) by Dirk Freder, iStock.com; baby vulture (question 9) David Sanders/Arizona Daily Star

Inquiries should be addressed to:

Pineapple Press, Inc.
P.O. Box 3889
Sarasota, Florida 34230
www.pineapplepress.com

Library of Congress Cataloging-in-Publication Data

Magellan, Marta,
Those voracious vultures / Marta Magellan ; illustrations by Steve Weaver ; photographs by James Gersing and Ron Magill.-- 1st ed.
p. cm.
Includes bibliographical references and index.
ISBN-13: 978-1-56164-424-7 (hardback : alk. paper)
ISBN-13: 978-1-56164-425-4 (pbk. : alk. paper)
1. Vultures--Juvenile literature. I. Weaver, Steve, ill. II. Gersing, James, ill. III. Magill, Ron, ill. IV. Title.
QL696.F32M2576 2007
598.9'2--dc22
2008008762

First Edition
Hb 10 9 8 7 6 5 4 3 2 1
Pb 10 9 8 7 6 5 4 3 2 1

Design by Steve Weaver
Printed in China

To my mother, Rita de Cassia

Special thanks to:

Brigitte Grosjean and Patrick Prentice of Jungle Island, Miami, Florida, for introducing us to the park's juvenile king vulture, Solomon, and their Andean condor, Señor Jefe; vulture expert Sheila Gaby, Ph.D., biology professor, Miami Dade College for her expertise; Tamian Wood for creating the activities; Elaine Landau for tips on children's nonfiction; Sid Kaskey for introducing us to the vultures outside his office; Danielle Joseph for discovering Solomon; Linda Bernfeld and the members of the Miami SCWBI critique group.

Contents

Cape griffon vulture

What are vultures?

Vultures are large birds that eat the flesh of dead animals, called carrion. That's why we call them voracious, meaning they have a huge appetite. A lot of people think vultures are creepy, but they are important to us. They help keep the fields, forests, and even our neighborhoods clean by eating up the dead animals. That's a job few other animals want! There are two types of vultures: New World (from the Americas) and Old World (from Europe, Africa, and Asia).

HELP WANTED EATING DEAD ROTTEN STUFF

Ruppell's griffon vultures

Why do we need vultures?

Vultures are important to us because they are like the earth's janitors. When an animal dies, vultures will swoop down and devour all of its flesh. In Africa a large flock of vultures can turn a large animal into a skeleton in a few hours. If vultures didn't exist, rotten flesh, eggs, and fish would lie around a long time, decaying and spreading disease. It's a good thing vultures like to eat revolting things other animals won't go near.

Lappet-faced vulture

Why are vultures' heads bald?

Bald eagles aren't really bald, but almost all vultures are! A feathery head would pick up unwanted pieces of meat. Vultures can stick their heads inside a dead animal without picking up too much blood or flesh. It is easier for the bald head to dry and for tiny bugs called bacteria to bake off in the sun.

Andean condor

Why do vultures vomit?

Vultures vomit (throw up) to protect themselves from predators, animals that hunt others. That's gross, but they cough up stinky half-digested meat when they feel threatened or when another animal gets too close to their nests. It makes their stomachs lighter in case they have to fly away really fast. It also discourages the predator from getting too close. Their vomit is not only stinky, but loaded with acid. If you got close enough to touch it, it would sting!

Andean condor

What other gross things do vultures do?

Vultures sometimes have to step inside the carcass (dead body) of the animal they are eating. That's pretty gross, but not as gross as something else they do. New World vultures urinate on their legs! The urine has a strong acid that helps get rid of the bacteria. It might also help to keep them cool. This milky white liquid makes their legs look like they're spray-painted white.

Lappet-faced vulture

Ruppell's griffon
vultures

What are vultures' favorite foods?

Like everybody else, vultures don't like meat when it's *too* rotten. Yuk! They like herbivores (plant-eating animals) like deer, horses, and cows better than carnivores (meat eaters) like dogs and cats. But they will eat them when there is nothing else. Some vultures enjoy dead fish. Others will eat abandoned eggs, insects, or juicy maggots.

Lappet-faced vulture

Eurasian
vulture

Why don't vultures get sick when they eat rotten meat?

Their stomachs are so strong, vultures can eat just about anything. When they eat decaying meat, the bacteria inside their stomachs digest it. They have a hundred times more stomach bacteria than humans do. That's billions and billions more bacteria! A long time ago people thought vultures carried disease. Now we know that because of their strong stomachs, disease-causing bacteria don't live long inside vultures.

Turkey vultures

Why do vultures circle?

When vultures circle, most people think there must be a dead body below. Sometimes the circling vultures are just searching for food. They could also be gaining altitude for a long flight. Some people also think that vultures will circle a dying animal, waiting for it to die. Not really. Some Old World vultures without a sense of smell wait for as long as two days around a fallen animal. They aren't sure if the animal is really dead!

Did you know that a group of circling vultures is called "a kettle of vultures"?

Baby king vulture

What are baby vultures like?

When baby vultures hatch, they are a ball of white fluff with a black head. As they get older, their feathers begin to turn darker. Their heads stay black for a long time like the baby king vulture in this picture. Vultures take around five or six years to become adults. Then their feathers will take on their final colors. And then they can lay eggs and have babies of their own.

Turkey vultures

Where do vultures live?

There are vultures on almost every continent except Antarctica and Australia. Old World vultures can be found in Europe, Africa, the Middle East, and Asia.

In the New World the king and yellow-headed vultures live in South America. The turkey and black vultures migrate from North America to as far south as Chile. The California condor is endangered and found only in a small area of California. The Andean condor lives mostly in the mountain chain in South America called the Andes.

Andean condor
female

Andean condor
male

How can you tell girl and boy vultures apart?

Most of the time you can't tell which vulture is a boy and which is a girl. They are so much alike in most cases that only a scientist can tell which is which. One exception is the Andean condor. The girl condor has a nice, smooth head. The boy condor has a big glob of flesh on its forehead called a *caruncle.*

Bird trainer Patrick Prentice with Andean condor at Jungle Island, Miami, Florida

How big are vultures?

Vultures come in all sizes. The smallest is the hooded vulture from Africa, which is only a little bigger than a crow (but with more wingspan). The largest is the condor. It can weigh as much as a young child, around thirty-one pounds (fourteen kilograms.) It has the largest wingspan of any living bird, a little over ten feet (three meters). The other vultures can be the size of a rooster to that of a large goose.

Turkey vulture

Lesser yellow-headed vulture

Black vultures

How do vultures find dead animals?

All vultures have excellent eyesight. They can spot a fallen animal from way up in the sky. But only the turkey and the yellow-headed vultures can smell. They have slits on their beaks that air can flow through (see the little photo). The vultures that can't smell follow the ones that can to the carcass. In the large photo a yellow-headed vulture has smelled a dead animal first, but the black vultures have taken over.

Hooded vulture

How do vultures fly?

Soaring is the vulture's specialty. Soaring means vultures glide through the air without having to flap their wings. They only flap their wings when they take off from the ground. Once they're up, they float on air currents (moving air). Most vultures soar with their wings straight across, but turkey vultures fly with their wings in a V-shape. Vultures can soar so high that sometimes a vulture will fly into an airplane!

Lesser yellow-headed vulture

What's the difference between New World and Old World vultures?

Old World and New World vultures are different in many ways. They look kind of alike because of their behavior (eating carrion), not because they share the same ancestors. A big difference is that the Old World vultures have much bigger and stronger beaks and claws. See list of Old and New World vultures on page 52.

White-headed vulture

Why are vultures always black in cartoons?

Vultures are always black in cartoons because people associate them with creepy dead things. Some vultures are white with black wingtips. King vultures have colorful heads—orange, green, and purplish blue. The lesser yellow-headed vulture has a yellowish head (surprise!) with a red neck. The Eurasian vulture sports a feathery ruff around its downy white head. The Andean condor has a ruff that looks and feels like a white mink stole.

Turkey vulture

Do turkey vultures gobble?

Turkey vultures do not gobble. They are called turkey vultures because they have bald red heads like turkeys. Like most vultures, they have hardly any voice at all. Vultures will hiss, growl, and grunt sometimes, but mostly they make very little noise. Don't worry. There will never be a turkey vulture instead of a turkey for your holiday dinner.

Turkey vultures
Miami, Florida

Are vultures endangered?

The number of vultures is decreasing because they are losing their natural habitats. Some, like the California condor, are facing extinction. Other vultures are doing just fine. Some vultures have begun to live among people, eating road kill or garbage. Many roost on balconies and the tops of tall buildings in cities. Still, like most wild birds, vultures need forests and trees to nest.

Black vultures

Why do vultures hang out in groups?

Not all vultures like to hang out in groups, but many do. Black and griffon vultures flock in family groups. Old World vultures group together around a fallen animal to eat different parts of the carcass. Bigger vultures with stronger beaks will work on the carcass first before the smaller ones move in for the leftovers.

PLEASE
TAKE A
NUMBER

Turn me sideways
to see my wide
wings.

Andean condor

Why do vultures stand with their wings spread wide apart?

Vultures are often seen standing in what is called a *horaltic pose*. Scientists aren't sure why vultures do this. Perhaps they do it to let the sun bake yucky stuff and bugs off their wings. Or maybe they just want to cool off, or warm up, or straighten out their flight feathers. Whatever the reason, they look cool doing it.

Make a vulture collage
Here is an outline of an Old World Eurasian vulture. You can put it through a copy machine and make it bigger. Make a collage with glue and bits of magazine paper cut or torn into small pieces. Glue different colored bits on the picture any way you want. If you have feathers, you can use those, too!

Make a turkey vulture mobile
Ask someone with a copy machine to photocopy the vulture on the facing page. Make sure you have thick paper. Cut out both vultures on the dotted red lines. Tape a penny in between the top and bottom of the body of the vulture. This will give it weight. Glue the top and bottom vultures together (the face and feet will be on the bottom) and then use your scissors to trim so that the wings are even. Fold the wings at the black dotted lines so that your turkey vulture flies in a V. Poke two holes, one on each wing. Take a piece of string about twenty inches long (or as long as you want) and knot it under each hole. Now you are ready to hang your turkey vulture.

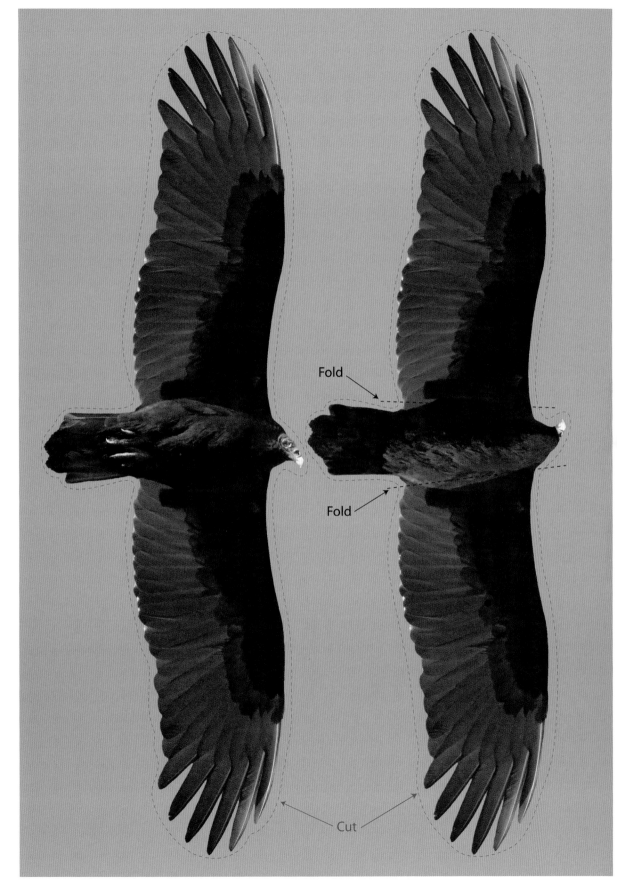

Fold

Fold

Cut

Connect the dots

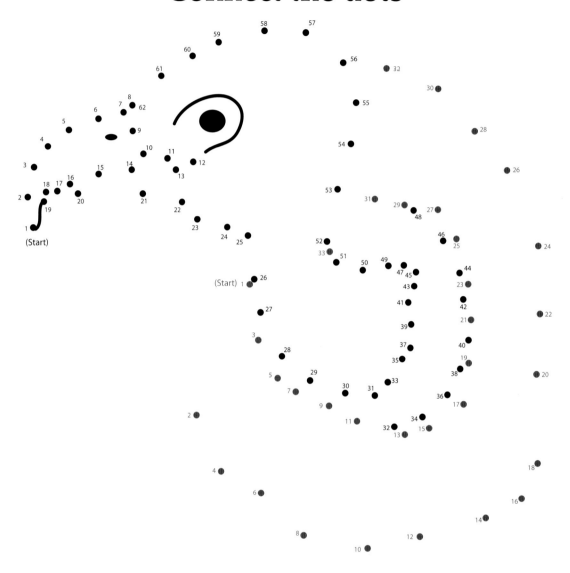

Connect the dots to find the unique Eurasian vulture.

First, connect the black dots in numeric order, beginning at number 1 (Start). Next, connect the red dots in order, beginning with the red number 1 (Start). When you get to the last red dot (number 33), connect it to the black dot (number 52).

This vulture lives in Asia, northwestern Africa, India, and Turkey, and has a feathery ruff during breeding season.

Where to learn more about vultures

Good books to read

Animal Scavengers: Vultures by Sandra Markle, Lerner Publications Company, Minneapolis, 2005.

Vultures by Mark J. Rauzon, Grolier Publishing, First Books, New York, 1997.

Condors and Vultures by David Houston, World Life Library, Voyageur Press, Stillwater, Minnesota, 2001.

Birds of Prey Rescue by Pamela Hickman, Firefly Books, Ltd., Ontario, 2006.

Good websites to visit

www.vultures.homestead.com

www.lairweb.org.nz/vulture/

http://www.birds.cornell.edu/AllAboutBirds/ BirdGuide/Black_Vulture.html

Kinds of vultures

Old World Vultures (Europe, Africa, and Asia)
Bearded vulture
Eurasian vulture
Long-billed vulture
Asian vulture
Cinereous vulture
Cape griffon vulture
Rupell's griffon vulture
African white-backed vulture
Himalayan vulture
Palm nut vulture
Indian black vulture (pondicherry)
Egyptian vulture
Lappet-faced vulture
Hooded vulture
White-headed vulture

New World Vultures (the Americas)
Turkey vulture
Black vulture
King vulture
Lesser yellow-headed vulture
Greater yellow-headed vulture
California condor
Andean condor

Glossary

altitude – height above the Earth

bacteria – tiny invisible bugs, some good, some bad, that grow inside living things. Good bacteria can help digest food.

carcass – a dead body

carnivores – animals that eat only meat

caruncle – the extra glob of flesh that some animals, like turkeys and vultures, have on their heads and necks

carrion – the flesh of dead animals, usually beginning to rot

decompose – to rot

extinction – when a species has died out completely

habitat – the place where an animal naturally lives and grows

herbivores – animals who eat plants, grasses, and vegetables, but not meat

horaltic pose – the way birds stand with their wings spread apart

migrate – to move from one place to another when the seasons change

predators – animals that hunt other animals for food

roost – the way birds rest or perch

urinate – to pee

vomit – to throw up

voracious – having a huge appetite

wingspan – the measurement of a bird's open wings, tip to tip

About the author

Marta Magellan is a nature lover who teaches
English, Creative Writing, and Survey of
Children's Literature at Miami Dade College in
Miami, Florida. She travels often to Brazil, Central
America, and anywhere else she can enjoy nature.
She lives in Miami with her husband, James
Gersing, who photographed many of the vultures
in this book. She is seen here with Solomon, a
juvenile king vulture from Jungle Island in Miami.

Index

(Numbers in **bold** refer to photographs.)

Here are the other books in this series. For a complete catalog, write to Pineapple Press, P.O. Box 3889, Sarasota, Florida 34230-3889, or call (800) 746-3275. Or visit our website at www.pineapplepress.com.

Those Amazing Alligators by Kathy Feeney. Illustrated by Steve Weaver, photographs by David M. Dennis. Alligators are amazing animals, as you'll see in this book. Discover the differences between alligators and crocodiles; learn what alligators eat, how they communicate, and much more. Ages 5–9.

Those Beautiful Butterflies by Sarah Cussen. Illustrated by Steve Weaver. This book answers 20 questions about butterflies—their behavior, why they look the way they do, how they communicate, and much more. Ages 5–9.

Those Delightful Dolphins by Jan Lee Wicker. Illustrations by Steve Weaver. Learn the difference between a dolphin and a porpoise, find out how dolphins breathe and what they eat, and learn how smart they are and what they can do. Ages 5–9.

Those Excellent Eagles by Jan Lee Wicker. Illustrated by Steve Weaver, photographs by H. G. Moore III. Learn all about those excellent eagles—what they eat, how fast they fly, why the American bald eagle is our nation's national bird. You'll even make some edible eagles. Ages 5–9.

Those Funny Flamingos by Jan Lee Wicker. Illustrated by Steve Weaver. Flamingos are indeed funny birds. Learn why those funny flamingos are pink, stand on one leg, eat upside down, and much more. Ages 5–9.

Those Lively Lizards by Marta Magellan. Illustrated by Steve Weaver, photographs by James Gersing. In this book you'll meet lizards that can run on water, some with funny-looking eyes, some that change color, and some that look like little dinosaurs. Ages 5–9.

Those Magical Manatees by Jan Lee Wicker. Illustrated by Steve Weaver. Twenty questions and answers about manatees—you'll find out more about their behavior, why they're endangered, and what you can do to help. Ages 5–9.

Those Outrageous Owls by Laura Wyatt. Illustrated by Steve Weaver, photographs by H. G. Moore III. Learn what owls eat, how they hunt, and why they look the way they do. You'll find out what an owlet looks like, why horned owls have horns, and much more. Ages 5–9.

Those Peculiar Pelicans by Sarah Cussen. Illustrated by Steve Weaver, photographs by Roger Hammond. Find out how much food those peculiar pelicans can fit in their beaks, how they stay cool, and whether they really steal fish from fishermen. And learn how to fold up an origami pelican. Ages 5–9.

Those Terrific Turtles by Sarah Cussen. Illustrated by Steve Weaver, photographs by David M. Dennis. You'll learn the difference between a turtle and a tortoise, and find out why they have shells. Meet baby turtles and some very, very old ones, and even explore a pond. Ages 5–9.